AF489761

THIS BOOK BELONGS TO:

May we so love as never to have occasion to
repent of our love!

HENRY DAVID THOREAU

LOVE

In love, as in gluttony, pleasure is a matter of the utmost precision.

ITALO CALVINO

Love will subsist on wonderfully little hope but
not altogether without it.

WALTER SCOTT

Love

"Love all, trust a few, do wrong to none."

WILLIAM SHAKESPEARE

"It is not a lack of love, but a lack of friendship that makes unhappy marriages."

FRIEDRICH NIETZSCHE

> "As he read, I fell in love the way you fall asleep: slowly, and then all at once."
>
> JOHN GREEN

"It is better to be hated for what you are than to be loved for what you are not."

ANDRE GIDE

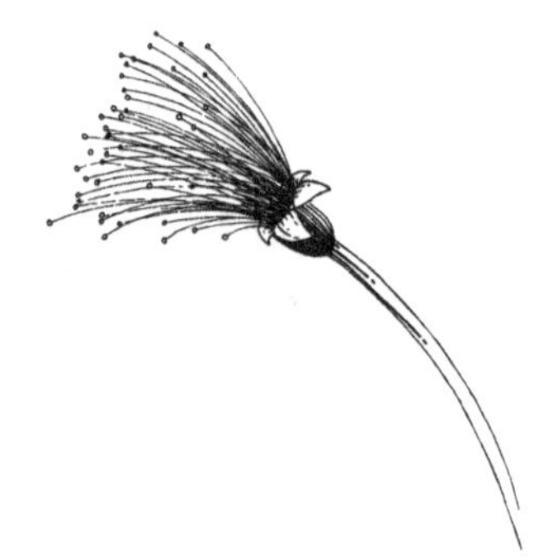

"There are many things that seem impossible only so long as one does not attempt them."

ANDRE GIDE

"We accept the love we think we deserve."

STEPHEN CHBOSKY

Just Color

"A friend is someone who knows all about you
and still loves you."

ELBERT HUBBARD

"You always pass failure on the wayto success."

MICKEY ROONEY

"No one is perfect - that's why pencils have erasers."

WOLFGANG RIEBE

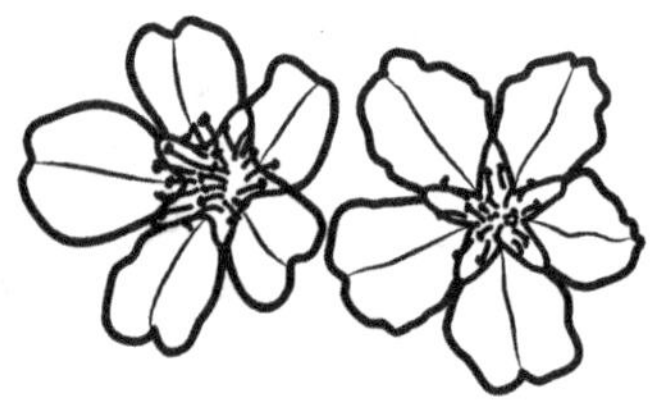

"It always seems impossible until it is done."

NELSON MANDELA

"Keep your face to the sunshine and you cannot
see a shadow."

HELEN KELLER

"The only time you fail is when you fall down and stay down."

STEPHEN RICHARDS

"Positive anything is better thannegative nothing."

ELBERT HUBBARD

"It makes a big difference in your life when youstay positive."

ELLEN DEGENERES

"If opportunity doesn't knock, build a door."

MILTON BERLE

"You are never too old to set another goal or dream a new dream."

LES BROWN

"It's not whether you get knocked down, it's whether you get up."

VINCE LOMBARDI

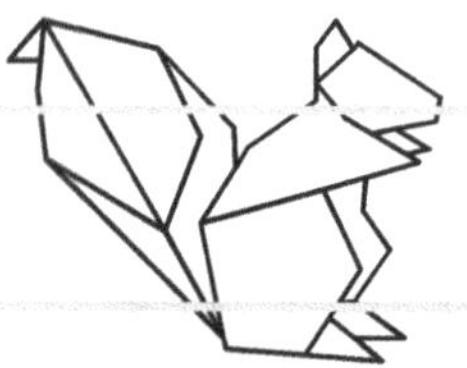

"Hard work keeps the wrinkles out of the mind
and spirit."

HELENA RUBINSTEIN

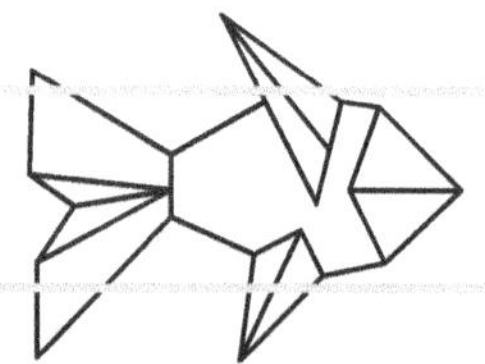

"Success is the sum of small efforts repeated day in and day out."

ROBERT COLLIER

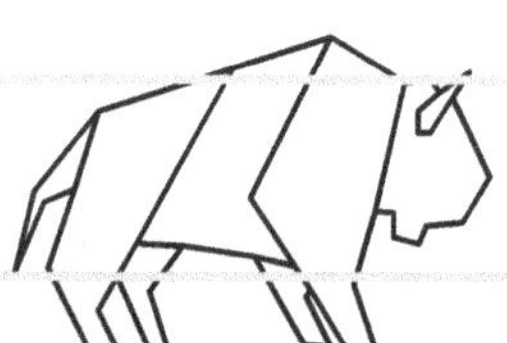

"Happiness is the only thing that multiplies when you share it."

ALBERT SCHWEITZER

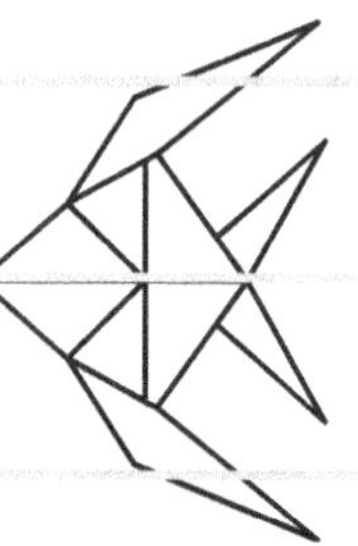

LOVE
YOU

"Live life to the fullest and focus onthe positive."

MATT CAMERON

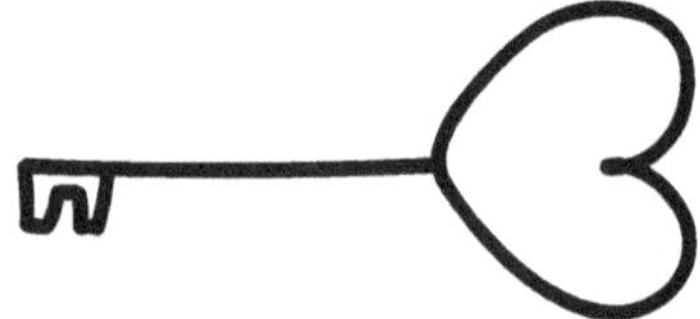

"The Best Way To Get Started Is To Quit Talking And Begin Doing."

WALT DISNEY

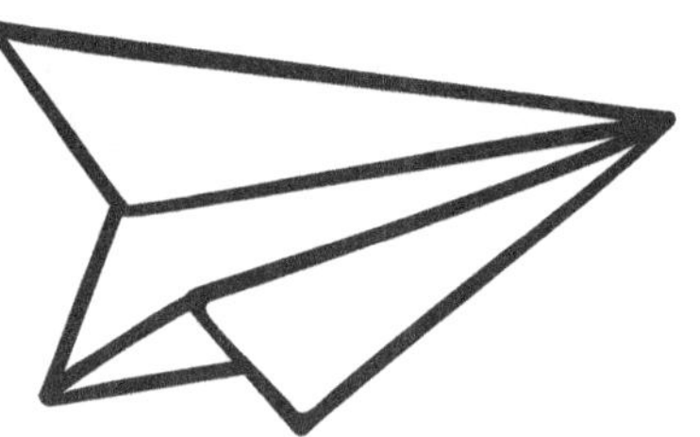

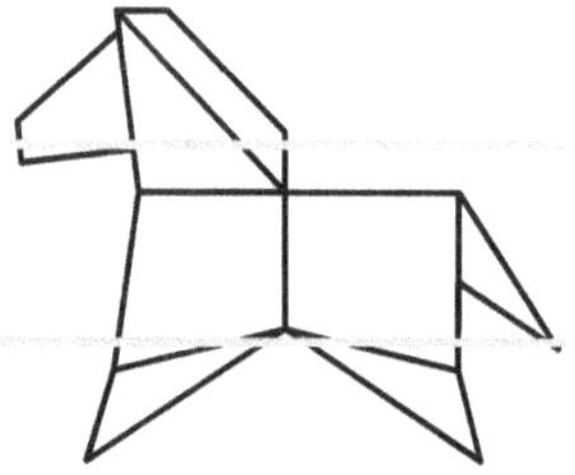

"Don't Let Yesterday Take Up Too Much Of Today."

WILL ROGERS

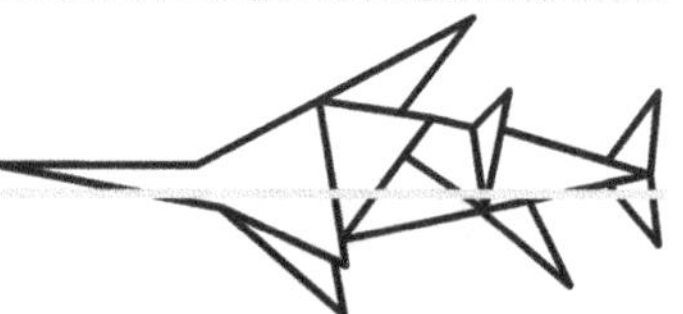

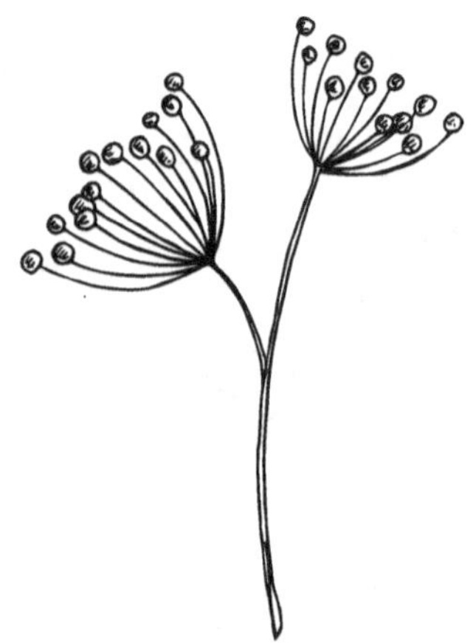

"Failure Will Never Overtake Me If My Determination To Succeed Is Strong Enough."

OG MANDINO

"We May Encounter Many Defeats But We Must Not Be Defeated."

MAYA ANGELOU

"We Generate Fears While We Sit. We Overcome Them By Action."

DR. HENRY LINK

"Whether You Think You Can Or Think You Can't, You're Right."

HENRY FORD

"Creativity Is Intelligence Having Fun."

ALBERT EINSTEIN

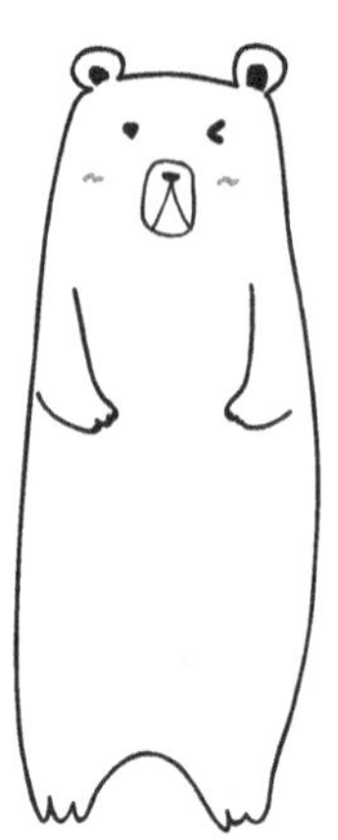

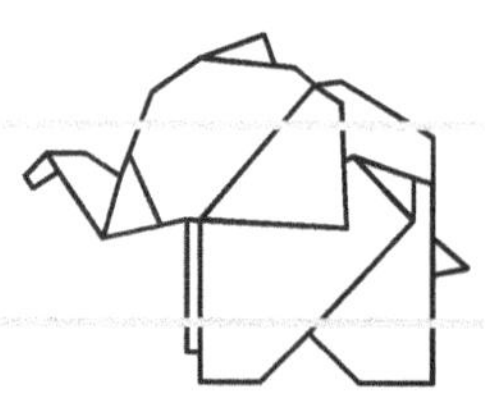

"Do What You Can With All You Have, Wherever You Are."

THEODORE ROOSEVELT

LOVE

"To See What Is Right And Not Do It Is A Lack Of Courage."

CONFUCIUS

Just Color

"Reading Is To The Mind, As Exercise Is To The Body."

BRIAN TRACY

"A Room Without Books Is Like A Body Without A Soul."

MARCUS TULLIUS CICERO

"We Generate Fears While We Sit. We Overcome Them By Action."

DR. HENRY LINK

"Today's Accomplishments Were Yesterday's Impossibilities."

ROBERT H. SCHULLER

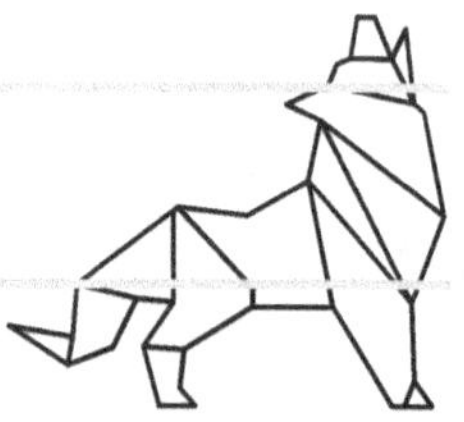

"The secret of getting ahead is getting started."

MARK TWAIN

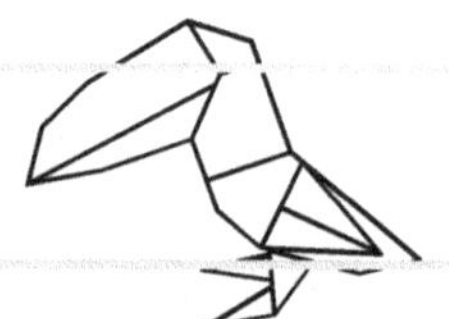

"Only the paranoid survive."

ANDY GROVE

"It's hard to beat a person who never gives up."

BABE RUTH

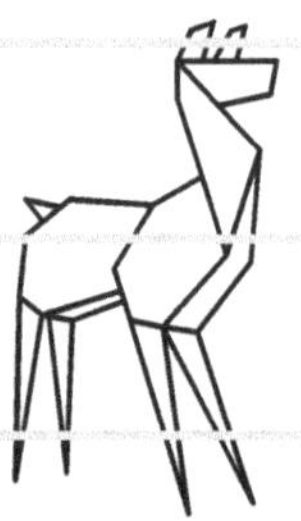

"Write it. Shoot it. Publish it. Crochet it, sauté it, whatever. MAKE."

JOSS WHEDON

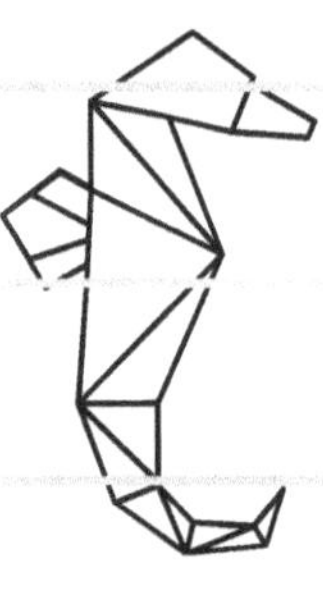

"Do one thing every day that scares you."

ELEANOR ROOSEVELT

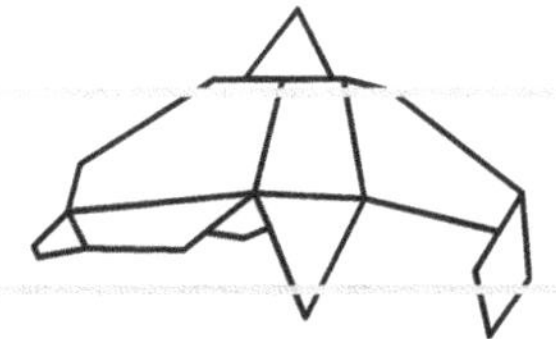

LOVE

"Whatever you are, be a good one."

ABRAHAM LINCOLN

"Impossible is just an opinion."

PAULO COELHO

LOVE

"Hold the vision, trust the process."

UNKNOWN

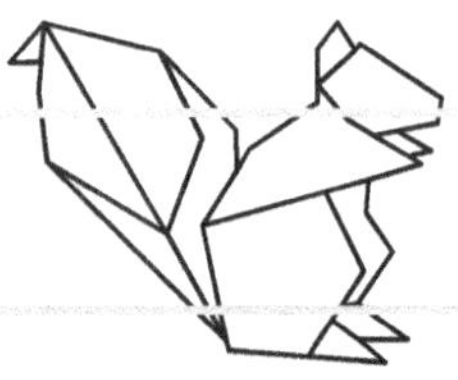

"The hard days are what make you stronger."

ALY RAISMAN

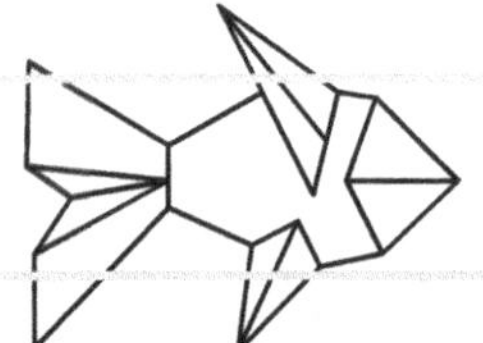

"In a gentle way, you can shake the world."

MAHATMA GANDHI

LOVE
YOU

"We Generate Fears While We Sit. We Overcome Them By Action."

DR. HENRY LINK

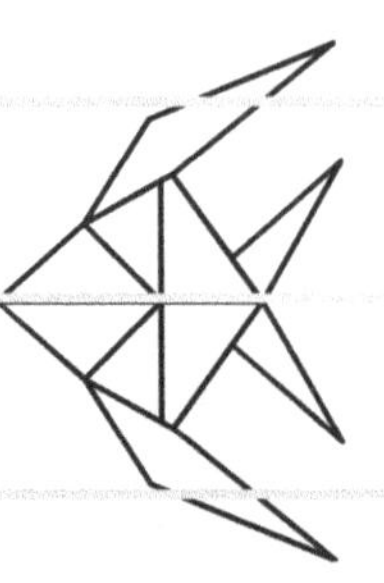

"You love me. Real or not real?"I tell him, "Real."

SUZANNE COLLINS, MOCKINGJAY

"Dream as if you'll live forever, live as if you'll die today."

JAMES DEAN

"Whatever you are, be a good one."

ABRAHAM LINCOLN

"Impossible is just an opinion."

PAULO COELHO